Footprints and Fingerprints

Footprints and Fingerprints

Lindiwe Mabuza

PICADOR AFRICA

First published in 2008
by Picador Africa, an imprint of Pan Macmillan South Africa
Private Bag X19, Northlands, 2116
www.picadorafrica.co.za

ISBN 978-1-77010 0787

Cover design: Flame Design
Typesetting: Triple M Design
Printed and bound in South Africa by Pinetown Printers

Contents

Africa To Me

(For Mabusha Masekela:
he at 10 years;
our conversation)

I prefer
no other continent but
AFRICA

each has its peaks
and rolling legends
chiselled by their own
blacksmiths coloured
in dyes of their own
oceans' roar and calm
but

I prefer
no other continent but
AFRICA

a vast question mark
for zealots of colour
dappled with Kilimanjaro snows
that have melted secrets
deep into its locked gorges

gorgeous with mediterranean capes
capped with
enormous mothers' breasts
for all creation's creatures

I prefer
nowhere else to stir but
AFRICA

hot cradle home of desire
constrained by periods
stained with sweat and particular
blood

AFRICA
serene love and bounty
honey that draws
with the splendour of silence
not birds that orchestrate
with wind wings and words
but lowing herds of
slithering stampedes
that braised and bonded her vastness
within the scorching exchange
within the bracketing embraces
of stone love at noon

but again
I nurse no preferences
but those heart-shaped platforms
where bronzes and browns
and all brawny shoulders brain

AFRICA TO THE FUTURE
AS LUSTROUS AS HER UNDISCOVERED WEALTH
AND WHERE ALL BRAINS
STEER HER WITH STEEL HANDS
TO THOSE WAVES IN THE HORIZON
BEGGING YES
TO UNCONCEIVED PREGNANCIES
THAT ARE ALSO OPEN-MOUTHED
FLOWERS

I PREFER
NO ONE CONTINENT
BUT
AFRICA

June 1976

Each Heavy Heart-beat

Each heavy heart-beat pulses still
Each heart of loaded centuries
Long buried
In the safe beds
Of these waters
Each heart-beat yet
Is living witness
To the freshness
Of our newfound
World

Each pregnant hill truthfully
Undulates before our eyes
Heaves
In languages
Fecund in shades
Of green truths
So that now for the first time
In our brief moments
The very horizon
No longer lures
As it once did, as it did yesterday –
Is no more elusive
For all now know
That we chose

We chased

Not in vain

For we have now tasted a victory

That nourishes our dreams

So all our tomorrows

Triumph

For our victory

Is the child

Of minds that master their own lives

Achieving what is divinely possible

Is our child

Yet our brawn

Yes our vision

Our brain

Now breathing free

You can touch it

Breathing so unhindered

In this place

Where all nature and beauty

Are stark naked

But like this river

Our nakedness hides

Deeper regions

Come now

See

This wonder close

Where our very earth

Meets

Those lofty blues

For us to see – for you

How contours

That were once

Very distant

Have been brought down

To levels that all may know

On our shores

Come

Hold our breath

Help us cross this river's

Steady unstoppable flow

For we have swum

In its currents

Emerged

Warm

All over all the world

For there too

My freedom was won

Come
Hold tight here this hand
It belongs to other dreams
That seemed forlorn
Yesterday

So much of pipe-dream
For sceptics
When so many patriots
Lost
Their youth
Their innocence
Their blood
Their life
Though not their spine
Chasing these dreams
We now hold
Across continents

Where are they today?
The cynics?
The detraction?
The nihilists?
The naysayers?
The prophets of doom?
Where are they?

It is time

For our merry-go-round

All around us

Thoughts breed new life

Geraniums

Suddenly

Pop here

There red, there white faces

From every window

Or balcony

All boldly saying

Let the world celebrate

Let's go round and around

For we too are free

To merrily-go-around.

August 1995

No Fun

It is no fun my friend
No joy
In the eye that blinks
From all these grim fields
With their predictable
Bumper harvest graves
Especially the children's assembly-line
In those black cemeteries
And the crude messages
Of apartheid slaughter
Between the lines of birth and death
It is no fun

Not at all funny
When suddenly every day
This conflagration of graves
Shapes questions
And the reasons why
Our young seedlings
This tender fruit of love
This softness of bone of brain
That even now needs a shield
My closed arms around
My full breast and heart
To give in all seasons

And the reasons why
This future is fertilized
With gun-powder
It is not funny at all

It is not a game at all
When explosives
Packed into some pieces of steel
Burst spread consume
My child's flesh
Burns then bone then marrow
Our blood waters
Their deserts of hate

These are no mere games
Of hide and seek
When children battle armoured trucks
Trap battalions with dare
It is no simple game
But war against
Hitler's sons and daughters

Soweto Road

On this spot rough
From cares of slow years
On these streets
Muddy from torrents red
On these crooked roads
Yawning for direction
Here where like early spring
Awaiting rain's seeds
Young voices stormed horizons
How yet like summer streams
Young blood flowed over
Flooded flower
In the dead of winter

On this road here
Here this road here
Tingles and shudders
From acid taste
The snakeskin snakestooth whiplash road where
    snakes' tongues
Flicker lick
Broken glass children's park
Road school for shoeless feet ...
Olympic track perfected
By daily daring sprints

Against passes
And barbed wire nakedness

This road pressed soft
Oozing like tear-falls
Treeless show-ground for hard-ware processions
All the June sixteen festivals
And their mad array of hippos
Muffling contrary anthems
With machine-gun chatter
Naked greed and lust for blood in camouflage

Soweto road drunk
From rich red wine
This sweet arterial blood
For choice Aryan folk
Battlefield road here yes
Here
Yes even here
Where road-blocks to life pile
Precariously
Here we kneel
Scoop earth raise mounds of hope
We oath
With our lives

We shall immortalize

Each footprint left each grain of soil that flesh shed
  here

Each little globe of blood

Dropped in our struggle

Upon the zigzag path of revolution ...

Soweto blood red road

Will not dry up

Until the fields of revolution

Fully mellow tilled

Always to bloom again.

July 1976

Energy: We Move

The steel-sound sounds of revolution …
they rise from the sweat of the soil.
where they land, fields of mushroom boom across.
over the frosty hedges of disbelief
the warm silent thunder of ideas
tickles like the first drops of spring on hungry surfaces
till with the pace of gazelles flung in motion
streams that were dormant bubble their energy
sparkling the hope of generations with ardent sperms.
beyond
from the ashes of our past, lost and now found,
new freedom songs whirl repeatedly.
we are not afraid anymore
as the will nods to the forward moving ocean
beaconing multitudes to peaks of granite –
resilient. colourful. and pregnant.

December 1973

Thoughts From The Pacific

(for Caiphus Caution Semenya)

If I were a song-writer
I would compose for the world
Ear-wax-drilling-lyrics –
Pound gongs,
Drum drums,
Centipede-legged sounds of pain,
Jut earsplitting wordspears to the hearts' brain
So the whole world can really hear
The feels of exile.

I would write of turbulent marriages
Between ourselves
And shark-warmed seas –
How like thirsty pebbles
We wait for some lone spray
(that never falls):
We come,
Smogdusted silhouettes
Acclimatized
Gravitating
Upon the hollowed axis
Of their timed, doldrum time.

I would also write of whirlwinds
Bristle whistles of challenge –
Unleash spiral bellows
Let their splitsplash fire
Their yoke of years
On Dawn's rocks.

I would write of the circled hands of
A continent,
A face of an Africa
Spangled with glowworm eyes.
Because she will reclaim her own
From these years' tides.

July 1971

Frankly Speaking

I must tell you
Quietly pointedly comrade
Jerk this limp will
Into motion
For this stream invites all
Though it also belches
Weeds and straws onto dry sea grains
Where eagles hover
But you will not see his descent
Through spectacles dimmed blind
By the spit of mambas
By oblivion as though you lost the 1961 vow
When we agreed
To suture firm the nerve
Taste grilled python
Defang the mosquito
Tame swamps to know your voice and smell our
    sweat
Soothe our burns among reeds and rocks
And the long march
To target this range

Lavishing on toddler's marrow
While you want to crawl
Below this slithering slime
To bloat your genius with its green
I must tell you direct comrade
You are your own liberator.

March 1982

There Is No Light

My father wears a light on his head
He says it is dark underground
His brother only laughs and says
There is so much light at night
At the power house, he wishes
It could turn into food.

My mother is at madam's
Cooking dinner on a gas stove.

I know I'll be punished at school tomorrow
Cause I can't finish my homework.
We just ran out of paraffin
There are no more pennies for candles
I guess I'll have to unfold my mat
And sleep.

Again we ran out of paraffin
Again there are no pennies for candles

Maybe ... maybe
Maybe I'll just ...

June 1972

Tired Lizi Tired

Tru's god Lizi
I'm tired
Washing clothes for
Forty years!
Sure clothes and labels range
Sure fingers chafe and bleed
Yes
– but little white girls
Don't never seem to change –

    You are so nice Mary
    You are the best
    Laundry-girl Mary!

Tru's god Lizi
I'm tired
Blowing these stubborn coals for
Slow winters!
Drains your body after a while
Cuts the heart cold! Lizi!
– then the complaints about
Wrinkles creases and folds –

You are very careless Mary
here, I have no use
for such things!

Tru's god Lizi
I'm tired
What?
What you say?
Ah! A letter from
My grandchild!

Lizi! It's summer over there!
They actually have earth
Like our soil she says.
America is burning!
Stores homes are burning she says!
Landlords shake insurance claims,
Black people just taking food
Clothes and anything brand new!

Hey?
What you say?
Makes no sense?
It's another world?

I wonder if she's tired already!
I hope she's not!
I hope she's ...

Yes, Ma'am!

June 1972

These Trains

Strutting, eating themselves
In pride, like a maiden
Promised marriage in times of war
These trains
I wonder where they go …

I wonder where they came from –
Gasping, spent yet still rolling
Like the ancient lizard's
Heaven-to-earth sprint
Bringing news of death and not life
To many worlds

These trains
I wonder what they carry –
Sweat in time
Lessons of want
Wrinkles of tears –
These are cars of steel
Forests of rubber
Mines and mines of coal and corn.
The gold of their diverse multiples
These trains carry.

It is a heavy load
The steel tracks tremble and squeal
Like the donkeys of old
Bellowing under the whip, whip, whip
Cowering under the strap, the strap, the strap.

The donkey gets nothing.
Nothing for the tracks
Except the pat and gloss of use.
The farmer, the digger, the builder
They receive the knowledge
Of work

    building
    making
    digging
    fishing

The farmer, the digger the builder –
They receive the shock
Of unravelling to their young

    no tuition this year
    no meat this year

      no heat this year
      no pursuit of happiness these years

They load and unload these trains
They stand stare and gloat
On the harbours of the world's wants
On the harbours of Africa's needs.

September 1974

Curfew

Stars
dance
and wink across the vast
blue platform of the sky

Neon lights
colour
the white cities
as hollowed
trains grumble
as numb
buses squeal
wheels grind
their talking
sparks
of stress and
strengths
on
the long road

As draughty dry sweat
awaits
each gray
smoky reunion
in Soweto
where

dust
dances and winks
across the length of sharp blades –
the ever sprawling vastness
of long thick bloody blue
and thin guts
far, far from
the white man's city

5th February 1973

Black, Eleven And Sterile

because your colour is your Jew
i dare not think too long of you

legs of ash
long, like winter's willows thinned –
thighs of black pools, want pooled
unknowing, thighs stained again and again
by banquets and banquets
of sickle cells of injustice
what shall i say
when you're grown
what shall i say
when you ask
'why mama, why?
did i menopause when you signed that slip
at the doctor's for the office of
equal opportunity ... ?'

tadpole bodies flowing, like reaching cedars pleasing
flowing reaching pleasing
hopping and bruising but always rising,
we saw you skip
we watched you at play
like some unbridled thoughts
we leapt with you with time

beyond the frenzied air of Nixon's grip

babygirl babysister womanchild

because your colour leaps

round and around like the yeast of jazz we swung

past the feast of satiated sharks

behind a diseased slave ship

this way and that way but always rising,

rising with battalions

from the heat-beaten stretches of Alabama

daring dare with millions

in the South of Africa

where little girls are unmothered at birth

womanchild

because your colour is your Jew

they will excavate the mines of your being

babygirl

because your colour is your Jew

because Hitler is a neon-bladed hydra

dare we enter your field,

warm,

dare we climax without tears,

consummated,

dare we think long of the shapes and shades of
    pumpkin

waiting in the flower

impatient for wind and sun and water –
in the spring of your truant yearnings
waiting?

i dare not think too long of you
because your colour is your Jew

not a word! not a word!
and he never said a mumbling word!
and then the operation
here was the tender skin
just below the navel ...
first the white doctor's eyes measured
then a surgical hand slashed
separating flesh from flesh
squirting blood from the reservoir of fresh warriors ...
the pomegranate chambers bleed the blood of green –
never again! not a word!
the little woman cannot feel herself recoil
as the doctor pulls and pulls and pulls;
up, up, up, ... there ...
dragging us down into
drunk ovens
leaping ovens
unchosen land

land-of-the-chosen land

choice uterus land

sizzling land that broils brains and wombs

land where children know death's labour

before the lessons of the moon

there ...

the hand that knows

the hand that writes

unleashes the best ties ...

an overhead knot here

a black-wall hitch here

perhaps a loop there (for the boyscouts of the USA)

to anchor the blooming lobes

into an eternal limbo!

there!

now each sperm must slowly knock

then die in our empty womb.

our virgin lands were ravaged and raped

the seed will not stir to dance!

womb of my race

target of their hate

womb of my race

forever they scrub you clean ...

clean womb, clean teeth, clean America.

and little black girls have paid the price

for the whitening of America.
and we here have paid taxes
for the pruning of the poor!

i dared not, not think of you
because your colour is my Jew

oh! the bitter screams of strangled truths
they hurt to the very womb!
oh! the daily drowning and draining
it calls for a major operation!
this foundation, time-eaten and festering
must face millions of fishers of justice –
it calls for a major operation!
these walls peeling off
cannot be painted over
they are storerooms of lead poison
this roof here can no longer protect
from men or beast or wind or rain
oh! the daily drowning and draining
'the whole jericho road must change!'

we dare not think of you
because the semite is our colour

yes! thoughts may dull the pain
but what we need are those that SUCK
the dams of pain ...
what we need are pyramids of hands to WRENCH
the belly of oppression ...
what we need is you, and you, and you too to RAM a
resounding NO!
to ALL in the world
who murder through laws!
who starve through laws!
who dispossess through laws!
who miseducate through laws!
who kill by giving drugs to children!
who institutionalize V.D. at TUSKEGEE for black
    guinea pigs!
who hate the poor for getting poorer!
who love the rich for getting richer!

what we need is you, and you, and you
to work for a world that is a fertile womb
yet always always pregnant for the best yes ...

June 1973

Embracing Exile

Yes
We drift
Country to country: drift

I move
Yes I move on
Upon, depending on
Ideal tides
But, even in the fashioning current

As it furnishes
I gather moisture
To carry me ashore

Sometimes too much
And then I weaken
From the weight
Also
Of blood and water-home, home screaming blood

Sometimes too little
As when it takes slow years
To rock
Again

Together in long warm embrasures of the sunlit,
   running
Sands

THERE
You can see
The piecing of wounds better
Than
You can pierce

A fish
High on its sunlit crest
Of awesome beauty.

June 1972

Home Thoughts

in our charged lands
    their cup over-runs with
        the sweat of gold and diamonds

in our ruptured lands
    orchards stream their nectar
        into resplendent European glut

in our lands
    heaving from heaps
        of dead labour

we mourn the death of peace
    also glorifying in the burial of dialogue
        for there is reason
           for faith's booming birth.

15th April 1976

Death On A Gold Mine

After miles of man-made volcanoes …
And then the educated explanations
Of piled, multi-dimensional piles of
Living deaths …
In the land of apartheid!

After centuries of dead examples …
And then the expert discovery
That the victim
Must be
Blamed
For being
A dead victim.

After all this and all that
In the land of apartheid
There is wine for celebrations
There are no more tears for libations,
For condolences;
No more tears for lamentation.

I am the goose that lays the golden egg
I am the heart transplanted to give life
I am the worm that ventilates the black earth
I am the kaffir that makes good manure

In the land of apartheid
No more tears.

Death On The Gold Mine

Twelve men died
On an African gold mine
The price
Of gold reached an epileptic peak
In Europe

This year!

Twelve months' labour exploded on a gold mine

Secretary of State Kissinger wore
A confirmation smile at the U.N.

Today ...

Twelve times twelve babies
Forever robbed of fathers
Twelve months of blood sweat
And deadly gold united in a splitting mesh
    From those quick on the draw

And Princess Anne's salary rises to $84,000
This year

Twelve women widowed bare
  Bare without rain
  Blood without gold
  Sweat without seed or harvest
  Gold without rest and glory and life
  Deep in a gold mine

Death For The Gold Mine

Only yesterday
There was a Sharpeville pitch
In Johannesburg ...
And all the sounds of the city
Congealed in a ripped faith!

Only yesterday
Our rising voices choked
In a symphony of terror at Langa
And all the sounds of the country
Congealed in a ripped faith!

Laws bound us
Laws exiled us

Laws murdered us
Only yesterday
All the sounds of the world
Congealed in a ripped faith!
And now,
Blood without motion on a gold mine!

Who shall raise the lowered heads
When black codes weave an iron grip
Around our wrists
Around our ankles?
Who shall home the child of the miners' dream –
This hope, this anger,
This vision, this march?
Say! Who will write and write over
The saga of a lasting people
Lasting when life winds
Like a straight-jacket winding
Forever winding to twist-in
The frail bits of nerves
Entwining with a pass
The saga of a people
Clear as the message in the black cloud
Lasting and moving on ...
Who will?
Tell me who will?

Death On A Gold Mine

Yesterday white-powered bullets
Deep-mined black warriors at Carletonville
Versatile skies concealed a bleeding heart.
Adolescent fingers jammed on the trigger
In Johannesburg
And the air could not shield
Against the predators' spotlight.
In the dark of noon
Manicured ladies eclipsed with their pets
The daily headlines of disaster!

Yesterday eyes spattered
Along concrete pavements,
Yesterday again boots drilled
Their swastika points
On open flesh and hopes;
Along bloodriver banks of white dominion
Our brains mingle with ant-trails and gravel.
Along the ridges of white waters
Our mangled bodies scream revenge on carrion rule
For twelve times widowed bare,
  Bare without rain
  Blood without gold
  Sweat without porridge

Gold without money
Deep in a gold mine

Death On Gold Mines

But there will be life.
The little flatworm reassembles
Into multiples again and again.
The voices of old
The voices of now
Urge us on …

'Pula'!
Rain shall sting the earth and
Death valley will learn
Natures' own generosity!

'Nala'!
Abundance choruses from
Sea to hill
And greed will know
Life's quarantine!

'Khotso'!
To the peace that must be

Forged before man studies
War no more!

Death To The Gold Mine!

But there will be life.
Forever the reservoir will generate fresh chords
And the heirs will distil
The waters of white ridges!
And the heirs will distil
The deadly waters in the calcified bones in the ridges
From the classes of minerals in strata of stones
From eruptive lava
From volcanic layers of mountainous pressure
Clean rain on round pebbles
In our continuous stream
Of ripe blood.

September 1973

Patchwork

(Baton Rouge, Louisiana)

Sometimes
Sometimes there is a
White rope
Around the hands of time.
The colourless hands of time,
The colourless hands of man.

Like a global lasso
Sometimes
The fibre knifes the mind
Releasing some young blood
And I unleash in my dreams
Spring gardens of my generation
Spring trees that bud and bloom
And fruit and seed.

No! No!
They didn't!
They didn't shoot to kill ...
They only want to keep me warm
For I feel warm now
Almost sleepy warm
In the company of the Louisiana sun

Softly falling on me
Quietly falling on the mouth
Of the gun.

Somebody!
Somebody please put grandma's
Patchwork on me
It's icy here please!
The blanket I mean!

Did she say,
Did she say at Orangeburg
The steel voice of bullets
Spoke through the soft smooth
Blackness of the flesh?
The students only wanted to know
Why!

Why the skin of education
Changed colours like a chameleon
Why so many
So many people in Vietnam must
Slowly broil in napalm?
Tender tendrils raptured
That night at Orangeburg.
People changed colours that night

In America.
Peaceful America sleep!
It's too warm here now
It must be the Louisiana sun
Almost sleepy warm
Yet the open air suffocates
Somebody!
Somebody please put grandma's
Patchwork over my head
It stinks here please
The mask I mean
Thanks.
Sleepy, sleepy warm now!

There were no rifles at
Kent State they say.
The students only wanted peace
The students only wanted to
Put out the fires that burn minds and bodies
At home, at work – abroad
Drenched in the colour of blood
Even grass refused to grow
That spring at Kent State
Even the air spun the wisdom of pain
That spring in America!

It is quiet now.
The dull taste for joy
Inundates my mind.
Now I am the fall in Jackson State
Shouting its suspect colours ...
Dark and red and gold and brown ...
Now I am the dark earth
Bearing on my back the snows of past years
Now I am the bloody waters
Moving unseen beneath the desert
Crystallising beyond the clean concrete
Of Baton Rouge.

Now I am the little sparrow
That disappears in the clouds
The dark clouds of aching people.
I puncture the clouds.
I render them asunder
Raining colourless seeds
Even upon lovers of the eagle.

I think I will sleep now
So that the grass can grow again
Innumerable as the wool on my head
Deeper than the puncture of my body
More brilliant than the mosaic of heaven.

November 1972

Corpus Christi

they call them barbarous murderers
those kings of old who washed themselves
in the warm blood of their subjects; those who ate
hot livers without gathering fire-wood where
the little person decayed, weeds and cows stood
watching power grow.

they call it the new dispensation
the kings of today who eat the bread
and drink the sweat of the victims.
as the desert crawls closer and closer to the disjointed
    hut,
can dazzling fingers of new direction
and the golden chalice of majestic destitution
bind all into one green ocean?

there is a place in the land of the cowboy. it
heals wounds of planes, those they earned
while digging eyes and splitting hearts of new twigs
in Hanoi. when they are whole again,
the planes lash the air with their fins
bellowing in lovely processions of death
far from the cleansing fingers and the grace of Corpus
Christi.

1973

Far From My Rivers

Far from my rivers always
Choking and bleeding from breathing
Drought
I stand on the banks
Of the Rhine so rich
So very rich

Every second
I watch with envy ...
Gallons of life-saving water
Happily glide away
To fill up overfed oceans

The Rhine gets fed up sometimes
So I'm told
From this unquenchable glut
Stirs up its dragons
To spread anger over land

Far from my banks
No longer able
To stir up
Their own legends
I stand on sands
Profuse with pirate prints

And sacred secrets
Buried in the belly
Of these pregnant scenes
Whose timeless beauty
Swallows our curiosity
Our finite musings
Along these waters that know
Centuries of confessions
Of anguish
And will always absolve
To give deliverance
And salve our humanness.

Voices That Lead

When we want to reach voices
Calling from the mountain top
And we stand at the edge of this abyss
Clawed almost bottomless
By the monsters' crimes
And our own looming fears
The mind's instinct
Will invoke each muscle
So that with the ardour of lovers twinned
Into priceless marble
Humanity's best cords harness us
Span us to resume this ancient march

But we must unshoe our feet
Let thorns and sharp clip splintered rock and shards
Bleed out our flatfootedness
Steadily
Till skips and leaps
Confront these hurdles
That launch the peaks closer
Beyond the mirage
From the plateau of deception
Alluring
A fang possessed

Some petrifying hiss under the rock
That wants to spit venom on our will
Bend us into submission
Or kill resistance from us
It is again those voices
That gird our loins
Enable us to sight at the crossing
The instinct mind
The parent life
The child
Our time.

Footprints And Fingerprints

(For Oliver Tambo)

We now know
With acute finality
That the profuse blood of your birth
Now and forever enriches
This entire land this country where your umbilical
    cord lives

Oh don't we also know
In the marrow of our bones
That at the appointed time
It beckoned you back home
From your unparalleled journey
To receive your last rites
So that the deaf the blind the mute
Can now consciously know and see and speak of
The hunger
The tears
For land rights

We have also seen that the cord was never broken
Then and now and forever
The link will never break

As each day
You grow and fuse with
Ulundi the Nile and the Ganga
One with the sky rain wind heat
Now in radiant shades
Arched to launch every one of our dreams
Pregnant with freedom seeds
Wherever your footprints
Challenge the sterile smoothness of sand
The humdrum drab of twisted logic

Your bold footprints will never be erased
With wind or rain or claw or other giant feet
But will remain
Tenacious
Deep in the core of marble
And wherever around the world
Your fingerprints confirm with will and
With the thrill
Of prolific impala horns
Calling
Blowing through
The thundering smoke of Niagara
Musi Wa Thunya
In Zambia and Zimbabwe
Contrasting

Harmonizing
With steady ripples
Of Scandinavian harps
Where such fiery hearts ensure
Soothing reverberations to your call
Till banjos accordions
Drums and more drums
Explode an ecstatic crescendo
Deep in the heart of Dixieland
As your conquering trail
Blazes the wild wild west
Rolls across Appalachian heights
Bursting Delta waters
Into the halls of Congress
Till the White House Reagan bull
Beaten
Drops limp
On its side

We now know
With acute finality
How you entitle millions
To our peacock bodies
For you
Just this once
Let us prance a bit

Let the unsung songs

Your life write

Bubble or sprout

In each and all

Let them raise our explosive plumes

So that the universe can see our new bodies

Perched on every hill or mount

Straighten

Then spread

This extravaganza

Allow millions

The right

Just this one time

To defy your modesty

And forever salute the maestro

From every mountain top

With the most spectacular SWOOSH and SWISH

Ever choreographed.

From **To Olof Palme's Sweden**

(After the Prime Minister's assassination)

I

I wanted to say
Today you know what we always knew
I wanted to say
Take our hand
Feel our pulse when it's not easy
But your embrace was all around
Already saying with your eyes
Between you and us
Nothing will change
Sowing calm and solace

I wanted to say
We know this moment
This goodbye without end
I wanted to say something
But you were already there saying
But how do you take this every time
When once is too many

So you do remember those
Everyday blood-pools on Soweto dirt roads
You do remember
New-blood Solomon Mahlangu

Young-blood Benjamin Moloise
The Moroka Three
Bullets piercing black flesh
The noose around soft necks
I wanted to say more

I wanted to say
Palme leaves you proud
Leaves the world torches
Then I wanted to sing PEACE
For this goodbye without end

I wanted to give you something
To swallow this horror
Just to say so loudly
In dumb-folded times
Our folded arms numberless dumbfounded manifold
    mean
We are deep inside your grief
It stings us more than words can tell
Because when the scroll unrolls
And those names are tolled, untold, but boldly
Written with his life his blood
Ask Vietnam Nicaragua Angola Mozambique
    Guinea-Bissau Zimbabwe
Ask ANC PLO SWAPO El Salvador

For answers in the golden name
Of this simple man – and –
They will say, singing they will want to say
The people live.

I wanted to say more
This
Today we know what we didn't know
We know what we must learn
From these comforting hands you extend
Today you wear this suffering
So serenely
Like that couple before the altar
Making their vows
For life to blossom
I just wanted to say thank you
For the son you gave our world

II

When one ugly paw reached high
The other opening wide its hidden breast
Housing utter pitch
The creature drew closer
Its fangs spitting cruel laughter
Then crunched the bulb

But this song also cries to say
An arm reaches out a hand holds steady
One end of the gun, its throat and its heart are one
A bullet of death that reaches out and

The report is heard in a dynamite sound in the
    breathless air

The light is out: the flower of futures
    slaughtered

As if hottest equator suddenly
Envied Sweden's coming spring
Sped its fiercest arson-squad
Scorched earth olive and dove antediluvian

As if the Baltic sluicegates burst asunder
Annulling every blade
Silt saturating every patch
Swallowing up what a billion Battleship Vasas
    couldn't

As if the iceage stalked every street
Glaciers glut seas
And when the blue heavens
Kindly sped rescue shafts

Tar and soot settled over seagull egg and seed
The throats of the wind syncopated
One deafening dirge
That reverberated over petrified lakes rivers and
    fountains

> Sometimes when one man is killed a whole
> world of being and becoming is seen to be
> aborted.

From **Elegy for Johnny Makathini**

'Look!' They say. The Sun Shines. 'There is our
   Brother and Comrade, Johnny' ...

It is therefore not difficult at all
No it is not difficult to picture
Comrade Johnny's last pensive smile
As he watches all of us now
From his new observation post
Stepping on platforms and stages he so well arranged
We can all see him now

Even see him squirming from embarrassment
Throw up his arms in the air
Over the beautiful send-off party, the funeral
'Why all this fuss Comrades?'
He the simplest of all

Can as well imagine him extremely attentive
Listening to all the well phrased superlatives
Around mission superbly accomplished
Hear the world's loving respect pour in endlessly
He would pull Jesse or Jerry or Nadine or Jack aside
As though for a pre-conference summit
Carve a deep smirk on his warm mask
Pout the lips a bit in a school boyish fake sulk

And when all are seriously on board
Chide 'But Comrades why use my name in vain?'

We can hear him chuckle roar or burst into laughter
And we hang on to the echo
We can see him smile calmly serenely
At the sight of all his comrades
So alike so together
Irrevocably bound with mother Mamane Valerie Nandi
The whole family and neighbours and comrades
Altogether for once together
All gathered in his Party's name

A youth whispers in church
'In the last few days
He worked extra frantically
Like one who had a serious deadline to meet
– An appointment with death –
Both arrived dead on time!'
Johnny still smiles the smile that is now ours for
    keeps
But he will also turn his head away
When embraces close freeze then shiver
From the same heart-fever
The gathering pain

All in his name
Your name Mfo ka Makathini

We are all here

We are all here
So we try to speak
Open our mouths
But unspoken words have propellers that urge what
  we feel
With a speed that overtakes logic
They are passionate grenades
In the hands of lovers
That split brain and all control powers
So pathos walks astare
Wears a sombre grace in the multitude
That ventures the last slow step with you But' Johnny
And for the very last time
You lead us in your hearse-house
So we can give everlasting testament
To a job well done
So well done we dare not only remember
How death's lashes come in flurries of a fury
Equal to slashes on bare backs
But know also how we must now come to celebrate
A love so fierce and undaunted

A life well lived in the service of the people

So while you lie in state, lifeless in state, still
Now in the galaxy of our supremes
The Semes Lutulis Brams Nokwes Mophoshos
And the lonely beetle buzzes
Its circles around the threshold
Echoing a forlorn song so muted –
In the body that shimmers sullen depth
And while OR's heart rests indented
On the mourning suit he wears
Grief defining his stoic face beyond the lining
As all can see that this bereaved father of us all
Sees beyond the lines he courteously receives
The deep robbery death has inflicted this time
To the course
To colleagues
To millions
To family
To the cause
But especially to OR personally
With the loss of this one

Son
Brother
Colleague

And Comrade above all

Still we know also that you have run the course, fully.

Yet … what do we do when such a spear has fallen?
Do we cry do we mourn do we shake ourselves
Into disarray?
Yes, we do feel a cold choke from such an easy death
Especially because we could not grasp
And halt and pull back the last gasp

We choke from many a lonely if or perhaps
And the awesome weight of the vacant glare
Of eyes swimming and drenched in pain
For this day gives new meaning to old words like awe
When we know tangibly and with all senses
That each heart you've touched
Stands not alone with himself
And even if alone
Still so with us because you took us there
And now all have become inseparable in this spirit
That exudes from each and all
And blends in wholesome filling strength
With your infectious optimism
Bound to our daily gravel

And now Magwaza we thank you

We thank your existence

We thank your being

We salute you

You have been so complete that we look back and
forwards

And

Altogether celebrate

August 1978

Helen Joseph

Even as a baby
Something about you
Must have been different
Without claims to superiority
The soft plump roundness
Of your cheeks
Prayed for peace
In their resolute gurgle
Right there in your crib

Today we met:
You were wheeled into our midst
Each silver-gray strand
Gracefully pulled back
To allow us full entry into your tenderness as
Your eyes would allow
Swallowing all
Into your infectious warmth

You came bundled in a quilt
Black Green and Gold
Made a simple statement
Connecting the past and the present
With possible futures

Your words have come to be forever
'We must move
From the margin
To the centre.'

Just King

(For Dr Martin Luther King)

We know him as yeast
Neither humble nor proud
Just yeast.
The magnanimous little grain reaches out
Stretches and raises lowly fibres of wheat
The lowly victims of wrongs
The magnanimous little grain moves
In unmysterious ways
Spreading mellow nourishment
To tired peoples' lingering yearnings and hopes
Tired people dreaming of a world where people
    flourish.

The magnanimous little grain embraces
Giving marrow and sinew to twisted limbs
Limbs brain and spine twisted corroded by laws.
The grain gives life
In the enduring sustenance of bread
Till many who travel that long
But not always lonely road of struggle
Feed then quiver just a little bit
From the riches to a moving consciousness.

Doctor Martin Luther King,
We also knew him as a hand
Perhaps the hand of the mind
That rubs soothing balm on wounded thoughts
Hands charged and tearing the veil
Of established fears and rights
Hands that weld together torn wills
Into mounting fountains of belief.
We saw the King build chains, people chains
Bonds that cut through the mountain of colour and
    despair
Revealing bare the time-eaten foundations
Of America's fetters
Inscribing in the soul of his nation an old law
Telling his nation
'The whole Jericho Road must change.'

Or was King a lamp
That shoots rays of warmth
On grounds saturated by the stench of colour?
Or was he not perhaps
A member of the new guild in the universe
A freedom guild
A guild weaving a canvas

That stretches beyond you, beyond me
Beyond us but of us
A canvas of superb rock brilliance
Anchored in the horizons of a world dream
A dream meeting with other worlds' dreams
There, where the best fountains sprout their resilience?

He was just a child
This little drum major for justice
Born to take up the ancient chant and march
Abandoned along bicentennial trails of injustice
He was a child nurtured
On Rosa Parks's strength
The strength of weak and tired feet
Black women's crying feet
Bleeding unfathomable hurt
Feet resolute about the peace of justice!
Just peace.
Just justice.

He was a child of history
Born to survive bombs of water-hoses
Fire bombs, swastika bombs
And the people survived.
They survived ravenous police dogs

Trained to trace black smells
Along marches, so many, many marches!
So many knowing dogs where people march!
Swollen feet do not welcome shoes
Although slavery taught us
All god's children got shoes!

We do not remember
What we did
What we said
When numbed by the news
Of three little black girls
Bombed to death
Death by fires of hate
In the church on a Sunday morning
In the cold, cold alabaster restrooms of the USA –
And their ashes spread –
Joining other ashes from other deaths
Blending to fertilize the soil of revolution
And the ashes spread
Untied to colours and land, and the ashes
Rallied souls for transformation
Breaking bars that slice faces
Firm prison bars
Bars of murdered justice

Spawned in the capitals of travesty
The monstrosity of capital
The monstrosity of super races.

And now as the backbone of oppression cracks
King lives in gathering crowds
Who are also clouds
That will mature into a thousand grains of wheat.
And now as termites plough the long trunk of the
    elephant
King lives in the lives of the fishers of justice
Who are also the children
That people must redeem!
And as the promised land
Calls in the distance
Those who were once hunted
Become the soldiers of salvation
Shaking hands with the spring of just ends.

16th January 1976

Tribute To Mazisi Kunene

(After reading his ZULU POEMS)

Where shall we replenish
if the springs cramp
from warfare germs?
Who will hammer the wall
between bleeding blades
and frosted minds of progress?
Who sings singers
that braid rainbows
with umbilical cords?

I could have adorned you
with Ncwala laurels,
but remembered;
desert aloes will always
flaunt drought's spears
with flaming tongues.

I wanted to build you
a stately monument,
then remembered;
monuments of our history
are heaped skullbone pleas
for flesh.

Wisdom-screaming pages,
we feasted a while in your shade!
Your mind led us to cycled
horizons beyond these.
There we sucked your breasts
then stored the rest for travellers
in heartgourds,
gourds that burst
into 'The Fountain of Mpindelela'.

June 1971

Climbing Mount Mapungubwe

(For President Thabo Mbeki and Mrs Zanele Mbeki)

If you have time enough
To stop even for a blink
At the burial home of their
Handiworks
Listen close
To that silence which
Amplifies
The joyous harmony
That awesome reverence
Of a billion voices
You never knew existed
In special hidden places
Because too often
Arrogant laughter
Mocked us
Trampling over our
Grace and dignity
With the brutal weight
Of mindless boots

Listen close
If you are not already

Confounded
By the flood
Of thoughts or questions
Already invading
This retreat into
The meaning of our soul
Our history

Step closer son daughter
Here into the home of their white bones
Where a solemn murmur
Perforates through thick mist
Hovering all over us
It stretches its multifold hands
To embrace
Your fears
The haunts
Of untruths from mouths
Always taught to denounce black beauty
But we are now entering
The arena of ancient wisdom

To suck every word
From lips of seers
Belonging to that reign of an invisible collective

Invincible

As patient as the oldest baobab

Which now

More than long ago

Has the power

Has the knowledge

To read in this weighty silence of the dead

Every single thought

Long before it

Shapes any tongue

To correct

All ills

Listen

How your heart

Paces fast as

That murmur increases its volume

As though we were approaching a hive

Busy on creation's

Sweet works

It builds up to a buzz

As the sweat on your brow

Down the spine

Streams

In some vain effort

To deluge every tiny pore
Our very breathing only
Because we did not
Offer incense
To announce this visitation
The same hum will not yet fully burst
Into your praise song yet
Though deep and high and wide
All over this valley of spirits
Your ancestral chant
Reverberates
With life enhancing rhythms of
Drums
Horns
Ululations
The thunder of marching feet
The birds brightly adorned
In robes
Of their love
From every tree
All over this land
Lend their throats
All saying
We are happy you remember us
Mr President

We will step away
Your heart throbbing still
For your entire skin
All your awakened being
Feels all these eyes
Piercing
Guiding
Every guard
Leading all our steps
Through these memory gardens
Where the blood and sweat of their days
Greets us
From each piece
Of porcelain
Crushed
Pressed
Now becoming a record
Stored
In the belly of this sacred home

On the second twist
Of this journey into
Conscientious
Conscience
We must pause

By the big fig tree

Bare

Or with buds

Always

Erect

With its serene promise of

Abundance

For we now

Step by little step

Learn of its power

To probe

Deep into our

Unknown self

For daring the spirit of MAPUNGUBWE

But when we all pass

The rope test

Precariously

Climbing

Balancing

Between a rock and then a slippery surface

To reach the peak of our search

Smiling

Grandparents of yore

Then usher us

Into their secret chambers

With their welcome incense smoking

As the brightest suns

Paint the valley

The mountain

The sky and its lacy clouds

Warmest scarlet

Because the first son

Of a nation reborn

Chose

Them

For his

THANKSGIVING

Here

High

On the altar

Of the golden rhino

As the whole valley below repeats your family song ...

Zizi Elihle!

Africa Speaks

If you dare
To open the doors of my dream
Take off your shoes
For these sacred chambers
Demand of all initiates
To kiss with bare feet
These very grounds
Bought over
Fought over
Bled over
With every drop
From the circumference
Of all seas
That encircle my being
The Mediterranean
The Atlantic
The Indian
The Red
Long long ago
Before the writing of stories began
For I am the fountain of all waters
Percolating ever over centuries

Who really are you
To ready for this journey into self

Take off the cloak of all your beliefs
Wear the mantle of a child in a schoolroom

Armed only with a slate pen plus
A burning zeal to learn the alphabet of history
Now being written from this point here
Where it all began
This cradle of a common humanity

Naked you must take the first step
Descend into the labyrinth of your new beginnings
Where the cleansing font of rebirth awaits your mind
    your soul
With its Caribbean Pacific or other waters elsewhere
Where generations of my offspring's blood
Have equally mixed
Under burning
Bruising heaps of
Hate and the total onslaught
Against Ubuntu

Under salt lashes and the branding iron
To give some in the world
Their claim to high civilization
Yes an even
Higher morality
Yet with lies
Rewrote my story
Recast my role
Reinvented my soul

But out of it all

I have come out

With a healing song

A poem that erects

The statue of peace

On commanding heights

The scars all over my body

Do not anymore teach me

Revenge

They remind me why

Never ever again a child

Of Molimo

Of God

Of Yaweh

Of Allah

Should ever have such gross marks

On soft inner tissue

For I am the mother reclaiming all her own back

To the fountain of new courage

A wisdom that makes you cry

With joy

Especially

In such times brutalized

By the poverty of mercy

From **Shanghai Suite**

(Our one heart)

If I should completely
Cease to breathe
Right now
Especially
After last night's tenderness
Please bury my heart
Where neither wind
Sun
Rain
Nor maggot
Dare to feed
On all such treasure kists

Because wherever I venture
In this tropical haven
Your heart inside mine turns
Each breadth of mind
Each breath
Into live cords that
Encircle my entire being
With irresistible
Currents

My charged body receives

Throbs

And writes back to you

With all the fire in my blood

Countless

Warm thoughts

So that

Beloved

Even in this separation

I am drawn

Tight to your baton

So that the tempo

In the pulse

Beats closer

Pulls hard

Drawing

To such pure pitch

This timbre

That defies

The Intrusions

Of curious stares

When we allow ourselves

To be spirited

Into a realm

Made
Just for us

Thus I now plead:
After delicious death
Rest our
New heart
In the labyrinth
Of some high mountain shade
Where it must
Triumph over centuries
Whose star-crossed lovers
Will come to
Measure how
Each weight
Each gram
Grain or atom
In our preserved mummy
So totally mixed
Bonding us into
Soul-blooded mates in this
Our one heart

For Justus Frantz

Yes
To Casa de Los Musicos
We converged
Like pilgrims journeying
To find their souls
After long long years' toll
On weary bodies
Harbouring
Some sacred core

From Bulgaria
Canada, Germany
Russia
South Africa
We arrived
In search of grace and other tools
To etch our new visions
Onto these
Here
Our new beginnings

We came
Matched by
Divine decree
For it is not chance

Not accident

That just us chose

To be chosen

By Gran Canaria's maestro

For as we must know

With finest print

Fate's indelible ink scrolls

Now

As it did long ago

On the Rosetta Stone

As it once did

All over the face

Of Aztec pyramids

For other centuries

To debate

To decipher

To dream over

With the eyes that ever are open to debate

Yes

We landed

Carrying bagfuls of hope

Our great expectations

That instantly transform all

Into the magic air of

Children's world

Where countless dreams interweave into

Miracles of

Acrobatic feats

Here

We negotiate our thoughts

Around winding roads

Each step

Unfolds new fears

There

Each sudden twist

And then another

Huddles us closer

When down we plunge

Holding our breath

Our brief breathing

Because our hearts are in our throats

We are cast

Deeper down into yawning valleys

Where all apertures

Open wide

To swallow

Yet

All remain on board

Bound by spells
From all those eyes of
All these sculptures
Where rugged carved
Cavernous beauty
Meets the very crescent of each truth with every
Dawn

We wake up

Like royal sentries
Jagged contours
Stand guard over us
Bid us stretch our canvas
To allow each ancestor
In each vein
To arise

Descend to these levels
To draw
Then seal
Deep traces of warm harmony around each union
Before that cool Atlantic
Sprays over all
Its early morning indigo

There are priceless moments

When every leaf blade petal

Incessantly

Teases

That helpless

Sun

Till from its mighty throne

It succumbs

To all that lives and swings

Down

On the ground

So much

Nectar

Honey

Yolk manna wine

Music

Now freely flows

From vast vats in Justus's Finca:

A conflagration of

Green hearts

Amongst red

Volcanic rock

Salutes

Architects

Of monuments

Overflowing
With bounty

But watch those giant palms close-up
How leisurely
They play hide and
Seek
With the heavens
Bringing them
So low we inhale
The promise of spring
Look!
Look!
Merry-making

They beacon us nearer
Ah!
The nimble fingers
Reach out
Brush
Stroke
As though on ebony
As though on ivory
Here and there

Dapple
Just enough colour
To balance
Moving
They stir
Caress
Entice
Every corner of
Our hidden being
Luring
Alluring
Tenderness
From our one gigantic heart
Painting all sensations
The same water-colours
Till we are arched enough
Till we are rainbow enough
To blend
Bend
To touch our commonness
Over one last canvas
Put our signature on
This blessed commonwealth
Discovered just now
When we bequeath

Each irretrievable moment
A little bit of ourselves
A little bit of prime-time
To this oasis of bliss
Justus endows our world

This is the home of
The Muse
Where we are
Pulled together by a magnet
We could not ignore
We dared not resist
For the vengeance of the Gods
Is total onslaught
Against mortals
That dare
Direct
The sharpness of their sword
Against destiny:
We stand
On very rich grounds
Where ideas
Conceive
Womb
Nurture

Living traditions till
In the fullness of time
They explode into
Philharmonie de Nationen
And everlasting ovations
To excellence:

The effervescence of music
Is infectious
For there is so much
Mellow grandeur
This full-bodied tremble
In the throat of the wind
So much self-giving
In this bird-haven
The pelican does not hesitate
To bleed
Its warmth
Its life
Shearing
Tearing its own flesh
Sharing
So that humaneness is reborn on and on:
We take off
On the wings of its huge soul

With benediction from festivals
Of Goldoni Mozart Handel
We ascend to the highest rooftops
So that with all humankind
Everywhere
We too come as close to the stars
And the Muse
Wills

Reaching up to the galaxy
We scoop enough energy
To fire ourselves
Into this century's agents
Not of Yesteryears's human bonfires
But of new worlds we create
Whenever together we
Hoist
Friendship banners
Along these mountain chains
With a haunting presence
For their wise eyes
Open us to the ancient soul
Of all such landmarks
Aligned to Robben Island
Which tears our separatenesses all asunder

Then draws
Then bonds
Our spirit into one
Triumphant whole
At the crossroad of time

Huddled
Along the edge of wonderment
Nearest the Milky Way
We also find fresh life
In the multiple language of our tongues
So that
With the world
We too sing
We are the children
Of this universe
Making itself anew
Thus huddled
We make the grandest entry
Into year two thousand
As family
This new millennium
Floating
On the ever so fluent
Fingers

These piano fingers
So firm
On the steady shoulders
Of one world of a friend
Justus Frantz

From **The Dosy Frantz Suite**

3. The Survivor

Because life
We now know
Did not spare you
The bitter taste of
Aloe
Now legend tells
Without bitterness
Without anger
A tale for all seasons

With every setting sun
Your courage grew taller
Than the highest mountain
Became an invisible shield
Against powerdrunk
SS troopers
Who stormed your house
Tearing afresh
A widow's wound
Still raw
Still bleeding from
Your husband's murder

Boldly

With razorsharp joy
They pronounce
Their charge:
WHY WHY WHY
Why out of a billion names
You dared
Christen your son
Born three months too late
For the father to see
To hold
Justus

Silently you pray
Justice be done
Justice will be done
Courage whispers

You swallow
Any faintness of heart
Stamp out any pity for self
Fix each pupil
Direct into the other's eye
Now that your spine
Stands erect
You take the deepest breath

Then
Calmly
Slowly
You call
The scoundrels'
Bluff
Face to face

'I come from a long line
Of lawyers in my family
Wasn't this the most
Natural choice?'
Then and forever
You remain a bride
To wit and to its wisdom
To bravery in the in-most heart of courage

With abundant grace
Making light every step
Along rough paths
Stoically
You soldier on
Counselling
All seasons
So much there is to know

Letta

(Mbulu, my sister and friend)

e contours dear sister
s we journeyed together
r birth before our burial
aders' horns blunted
rob vultures their sight
e contours dear sister
ns we surveyed together
rob vultures their right
utcast death escalates its slow tango
womb

r child
e peeped into my soul

red the launching peak of my dream
you have proffered your enchantments
I succumb fully to the call in the song
vith succulent hills, with the clicks of the

vices of the green valley flooded
mmer and water,
gs of the mountain, the peaks
l beckon, caress, beacon, command all at once
e dear sister the contours of our childhood,

And Fingerprints

Of simple
Green truths
Buried deep in the timeless
Flourish
Of evergreens

For what mother
Can survive
Unscathed
Through the living death
Of her own pretty girl child
Or two

Every day
Floating in a real Limbo
Lost in the unfamiliar world
Where death
The illusive guest
Plays hide-then-seek
To delay
The inevitable!

Bound to the wheelchair
You are no prisoner
To any handicap

So high your boundless
Spirit shoots
Freely
Easily mingling
With stars
In the galaxy of
Your own origin
Often catching
Falling ones
And then landing
Back on this earth
To swing
Twirl
Swirl around
To those hot
Spanish
Moorish
African
Polyrhythms
While youngbloods
Are left panting
Heavily
Spent
For nothing could ever burn out
Tarnish or
Unhinge

A genuine spring
Guaranteed resilier
By life

Through you
Slowly we learn
It is only when
They have been cast
Into the fullest cycle
Fierce
Fearsome
Flames
In the lowest depths
Where alone
With bare hands
For very very long
Duelling
Adversity's blazing
Many-pronged
Spikes
That true masters
Emerge
Steeled
Burnished
Emboldened
Beacons of hope

Letter To

(for Letta

Retrace t
Of terrain
Before ou
Count in
Lest they
Retrace t
Of terrain
Lest they
Before o
Over ou

For siste
You hav
There
Discove
And so
So that
Filled
river
The cre
With s
The cr
And al
Retrac

Our journeys,
The terrains that we travel together
Come once more
Wrap us in the warm bundle
The daily rainbow of the song
Water and light in an abundance of radiance
Haunting the blood, ineffable
Undeniable

Loose us in the wind sister
Lose us in the dew so
Our faces dance away the wrinkles of pain
As we loosen the seed in each uttered sound of your
    song
As we loosen the seed in each utter song
Sounding our depth
The skin of the seed wrinkles in liquid laughter
We burst into colour of root
And we drink the water of music
We break into colour of stem and are thrust
In the earth of your words
We unfurl into colour of leaf and thirst
For the light we breathe in your air
Flowers explode in the vocal volcano of your silences:
The verbs and verse of your singing quicken our fruits
Move us into ripeness

We listen to the wind
You whisper
We sup fresh dew
The wind sifts the water
We sip the wind
It is all there in your throat
The wind and the weather
The colours of dew in the early morning
The puzzles of mist:
The wrinkles of childhood

Weeds, chaff, deadwood and prickles all
Discarded
Now
Thus
Still
Mould
Ceremonial rites
Sister how you retrace terrains of our times and our
time –
Now

Now if you puzzle why I need to share with you your
soft

Breath in its sudden

Explosions right now afar so far

Inside my bone, my marrow with deep

Sensation that runs its river along my blood

With this delicious

Torture

Your flourishes, broadcast yes yesterday broadcast

Broadcast today

I say sister child if

You do as I softening sometimes quest question quest

Questions

Then linger for our world's long answer

Song sows us sisters sister

Songs sow us so

There are some songs stir birds to storm their cages

Songs too that orbit our brief

Breathing, our mortal moment

Into regions where stars also are mortal but always

Grow shining.

These songs are compact with the talking mountain
    springs

Allies of spray's melodies and they buckle the heart,
    they

Weave the brain away from disarrayed wobbling

In predawn nightmare

The songs make pact with fire, are disciples of
     strength,
Of endurance
They are in alliance with freedom, with necessity,
With discipline
They have the grace of water, the fibre of ebony, its
     timbre
And the baobab's
They upspine the knee, they buckle the back and the
     heart.

These songs sculpt the face in their hands and on the
     tongue
They taste the salt and smooth deepness, convulsive,
     of
Seathings, the sweetness of the nectar of flowers,
They are viscous and acid and tart and sticky as resin,
And fluent as wind and water and sigh over the
     world,
The world over:
These songs are our earth, our shape shaping us,
The landscapes of our birth, our labour, our travels.
You retrace the terrains of our day, so singing
Our earth's seething.

And so I boomerang back to you
Thus I will not falter
From the earth that you survey with vowels and
consonants
From the dew and the rainbow that you raise in
vocables
I drink the spirits of yesterday, I draw sustenance of
Ancestors
I find out how they and our children mastermind for
us
The future
In your present
Song
Your song which writes me long letters and cautions
And an elemental wisdom and histories
You have visited fountains
Now there is such music in the air
Such grace such benediction so much such music in
the air
When you retrace the contours of our country's face
Sow dear sister
Sing
You sing our lives, their reverence.

The eagle hovers,

The workers sing in the fire of sweat

The eagle hovers,

The nerve is firmly sutured

The wind is dawn

Where the eagle hovers

We bathe in the laughter of moons

We bathe in the sun's laughter

Where the eagle hovers

Where the worker harvests his fire

His laboured-for furrow, his blazing future.

The winds are wheels in motion

Though the dew is windless

The mushroom showers

And the rainbow.

We dance in the whirl

Where the wind hovers

The earth sings in its revolution – It is time – You
remember

For us our measure

You remember for us our measure

Where bodies become their music

The rock paintings starlight in the years' stages

Surveying the body of our nation

Sister retrace the terrains of history

Your song sews the hems of fresh horizons

That clothe us in dawn wave and dream tide,
And also where there are no stars.
Whirling
The wind carries new ululations
Harbinger axes
And one huge ocean.

It is break of day: dawn time
It is morning
The cock crows the life of distant rumours
Now
Long distance runners
Assume their posts, their roles, their batons
Miles of patient waiting are waves
Of running
The lovers relay
Our races our race
To the bursting climax
Human
Your voice is peace.

Sing sister
Sing.

December 1983

Do You Recall?

Beloved
Do you recall
Sometimes
Our first meeting
Only meant to be business
Over dinner
Do you recall
Though we were complete strangers
So close
So freely
We converged in conversation
We were born together
Except for colours
Except for textures

It wasn't long before
I suspected
We were both victims of
Umzwangedwa
This soft throbbing power
No one else but you can feel
Knocking on each wake up call
Consuming
Down to the deepest root
Of every breath
A beginning rare

Powerful
Overpowering
So very present
We were twins
Except for mother tongue
Except for fatherland

You must recall
Those days followed by banquets of
Bliss
When no dish could ever satiate
When between who's who guests
Musical beauties and pinotage
Our hearts defied protocol
Stripped bare
For all to watch
As lithe limbs
Coiled
Floated all over

Whispering to each other
Together we have been in the crucible
Have passed tough trials
And are now free
So guileless
So spontaneous

We are Siamese

Except for the geographies of our pain

Their diverse paths that bought us

This glory of our search's end

Twins emerging

Merging

And the twin searches ending.

There Are Spaces

There are spaces
In all of the closeness
You and I create
There are spaces
Awaiting their own
Fulfilment
In the moment of
Highest awakening

I dare not again doubt
The preciousness of your gift
Offered each time each time
The soul of your music
Draws mine
Nearer and nearer
Awake
To take
To wed
The baton of your heart

In the pulse of our
Wonderings
The musings of the past
Insinuate their
Bitter life
With their sweet hollow promises

But since you promise no paradise
Except the one we
Build together
Every day passing is a new marvel
Anchoring desire
With the tenacity of
Willow roots
Unbreakable even
Nearest the fluidity of
Their water home

Because of this
I have neither
Sulked nor wept
As each often must walk away
For though I've hated each parting
And the miles between us
I have also savoured
Every treasure stored
From which I quietly
Draw some
Naturing
Holds nurturing
And some maturing
Until the next
Honeymoon

The Day You Left For L.A.

When we meet again
Time will nod her empathy;
I will anchor my heart
on your shores
for centuries of nights;
dive into your eyes
for clusters of joy;
together watch temperatures spiral
with the succulence of love.

Then we shall spread
the tapestry of our bodies.
It will float over a burning candle
beyond the valleys of chiming stars.
They will make bricks of flying ash.
Your compass will guide
as we sing of a million worlds.
Then we shall know that love
is also made of the world.

9th May 1971

As I Remember You

Touch the mirror

Of my skin

Again

Watch if happiness won't embrace

Complete

Surrender

See

The nerves of our fingertips struggle

Inseparable

Our body bound for parables of dance

As burning lips send

Signals from this peak

For the erection of temples also

Along the slopes of sleep

In the springs of time the fields

Lave and lavish their breasts

Naked dreams stretch

Out to reach the rain

And the power of thunder

And the splendour of generous lightning

And the powder of hail

Storms hail your tenderness

Within the bowels

And into heaven

The propelling
Moment
Is so deep and distant

That we are eclipsed
And this is ecstasy
Which is the final meaning
Of our calm
Sleep ...

August 1981

Delicate Sparks

Thunder and rain clouds
That only yesterday hung ominously
Over distant horizons
Now quake quiver and shake
Roots of stars
Oh so many so-many angled sensations
In the hidden earth of my blood
Where bubbles brew home music
So long forgotten
Because long lost
But now they shimmer and
Simmer
Fizzle delicate sparks up and down
Their mellow freshness
The length of warm limbs
As nipples sprout
Because the suffusion of rushing tributaries
Along the thickness of African lips
Makes this birthday union the unparalleled kiss
That it is
Now and forever
Where all flesh swells
Subdued thoughts overflow
As we watch our litheness coil into another
While more heat fuses lasting relish

Deep inside the womb
Where each chamber like the heart
Flings bare and wide all entrances
So that our little death
Throbs utter benediction so poignant
Each surrender is fulfilment
When finally we waken to the tender leaves
Each leaf taking leave coming awake to
The giving of our once succulent body.

August 1991

When Hostility Reigns

There is so much
Such steady assault
Along the walls of my heart
Such bangings scratching such strikes
Where chips mount in pathways
Till flying debris detours
To those closest
As might pierces
So harshly sharp
So persistently
Till the barrage echoes hate
Round and around the hounded vault of the mind
Knocked dizzy
Until after some downpour
Short-span relief comes
Before again the quiver and tremble
From salt-water whip-lash
Over yesterday's malignant scars

There are people who play darts
Direct on boards
Live with nerves
Because the stakes seem so high
They poison the tip
Before the great witch-hunt
For targets steeled of mind and will

And those time-tested
Corrosion resistant principles
Then take meticulous aim
Pull hard
Gloating
In the squirt
Of warm red blood

But darkness will not shelter
Mischief and ill-will forever
For humanity's humane spotlight
Has rays that defy the darkest clouds
For how long can today's plum fig
Be saved
From the cluster of squirm
Entangled in the hidden core

28 December 1991

Peace Monument

Because freedom mirrors as it often will
The bloody faces
So many disconnected parts of murdered Innocence
We are charged now even more
To extend ourselves evermore
To create that monument of peace
To rest those many wandering souls
Their scattered bones
All down below remembrances
Akin to every shimmering of this Rhine
When neither ship nor fowl nor human
Can
Disturb its marble face

Even though night might haunt
Somehow it also nibbles away distances
When the forlorn full-moon watches
As moving clouds
Bathe the warm silver

28 October 1996

Acknowledgements

The following poems in *Footprints and Fingerprints* were
first published in the collections listed below:

From, *Letter to Letta* by Lindiwe Mabuza,
    published by Skotaville Publishers (1991).

Energy: We Move
Thoughts From The Pacific
There Is No Light
Tired Lizi Tired
These Trains
Curfew
Black, Eleven And Sterile
Embracing Exile
Home Thoughts
Death On A Gold Mine
Patchwork
Corpus Christi
From Elegy For Johnny Makathini
Just King
Tribute To Mazisi Kunene
Letter To Letta
The Day You Left for L.A.

From, *Voices That Lead* by Lindiwe Mabuza,
    published by Vivlia (1998).

Far From My Rivers
Voices That Lead
Footprints And Fingerprints
From To Olof Palme's Sweden
Helen Joseph

From, *Africa to Me* by Lindiwe Mabuza,
    published by Peter Hammer Verlag (1998).

Africa To Me
Each Heavy Heart-beat
No Fun
Soweto Road
Frankly Speaking
As I Remember You
Delicate Sparks

Of simple
Green truths
Buried deep in the timeless
Flourish
Of evergreens

For what mother
Can survive
Unscathed
Through the living death
Of her own pretty girl child
Or two

Every day
Floating in a real Limbo
Lost in the unfamiliar world
Where death
The illusive guest
Plays hide-then-seek
To delay
The inevitable!

Bound to the wheelchair
You are no prisoner
To any handicap

So high your boundless

Spirit shoots

Freely

Easily mingling

With stars

In the galaxy of

Your own origin

Often catching

Falling ones

And then landing

Back on this earth

To swing

Twirl

Swirl around

To those hot

Spanish

Moorish

African

Polyrhythms

While youngbloods

Are left panting

Heavily

Spent

For nothing could ever burn out

Tarnish or

Unhinge

A genuine spring
Guaranteed resilience
By life

Through you
Slowly we learn
It is only when
They have been cast
Into the fullest cycles of
Fierce
Fearsome
Flames
In the lowest depths
Where alone
With bare hands
For very very long
Duelling
Adversity's blazing
Many-pronged
Spikes
That true masters
Emerge
Steeled
Burnished
Emboldened
Beacons of hope

Letter To Letta

(for Letta Mbulu, my sister and friend)

Retrace the contours dear sister
Of terrains we journeyed together
Before our birth before our burial
Count invaders' horns blunted
Lest they rob vultures their sight
Retrace the contours dear sister
Of terrains we surveyed together
Lest they rob vultures their right
Before outcast death escalates its slow tango
Over our womb

For sister child
You have peeped into my soul
There
Discovered the launching peak of my dream
And so you have proffered your enchantments
So that I succumb fully to the call in the song
Filled with succulent hills, with the clicks of the
    river,
The crevices of the green valley flooded
With summer and water,
The crags of the mountain, the peaks
And all beckon, caress, beacon, command all at once
Retrace dear sister the contours of our childhood,